HealthyER You
Project

Develop Your Mind and Body
to Live Life at a Higher Level

Sondra!
Thankyou for
your love &
support!

♡ Stephanie

HealthyER You
Project

Develop Your Mind and Body to Live Life at a Higher Level

STEPHANIE BURGOS, MD

HealthyER You Project

Published by Purposely Created Publishing Group™

Copyright © 2018 Stephanie Burgos

All rights reserved.

Cover and Bio Photos by Nate Robinson Photography. You can connect with him on Instagram @ucfnate

Printed in the United States of America

ISBN: 978-1-948400-37-4

Doctor Stephanie Burgos books and products are available through online book retailers. To contact Dr. Stephanie Burgos directly, email: healthyerdoc@gmail.com.

This book is first dedicated to God, my CEO who has guided me and blessed me beyond measure. To my Mom and Dad for their unconditional love, always believing in me, pushing me to reach for the stars and telling me that with hard work, you can accomplish anything. To Luc, my life partner, my best friend, and my soul mate. Without your unconditional love and support, so much of who I am today would not exist. To my brother Chris, I believe in you so much! I love you and thank you!

And to you, the reader.
You are not broken but absolutely beautiful with so many gifts to offer the world. Embrace your beauty, believe in yourself, and go out and LIVE a life with no regrets!

Table of Contents

Introduction

The words in this book were inspired by my own personal journey to self-acceptance and self-love. Let me share a little bit of my story.

Since I was a child I battled with my weight. As a Latina, I was blessed with curves that I struggled to love into adulthood. In high school, I followed Weight Watchers along with my mother and lost some weight. However, during my freshman year of college, I gained 30 pounds and was at my heaviest. I was frustrated and disappointed in myself. I remember one vivid incident when I was in a fitting room at Nordstrom's and nothing I tried on fit me. I recall falling to the floor crying and feeling ashamed. My mother came up to me and said, "Well Stephanie, you know what you need to do, you need to eat well and exercise." I decided at that moment that I would work hard to lose the weight. In college, I spent my summers losing the weight and worked on maintaining the weight loss during the school year. My strategy worked and I lost 40 pounds by the end of my senior year of college.

Medical school came next along with new stresses and obstacles. I turned to food again to cope with my emotions. I kept up my exercise routine but the weight slowly came back. Residency was next and one day I reached a breaking point. I stared at a closet full of clothes that did not fit me and I said: "Enough is enough!" I was not happy with my size and it was time to make a change! This was during my third year of residency and I was tired, overweight, lethargic, and my self-esteem was low.

It was at that time that I made some serious mindset shifts and changes to my nutrition, exercise and overall wellness practices. Those changes are what I share with you in this book. Wellness is not just physical but also mental, emotional, and spiritual. Everyone's wellness journey is personal but you must set intentions every day to make it a priority.

I felt called to write this book because as an Emergency Medicine Physician I see all too often what happens when we do not care for our bodies and make our wellness a priority. I see diseases like heart disease, high blood pressure, diabetes, strokes, fibromyalgia and so many other diseases that are preventable with proper wellness practices. These health conditions and concerns I am seeing in adults, teenagers and children drive me to do this work. I am tired of seeing so many young people affected by conditions and diseases that used to only impact us as we got older. We MUST take control of our health and understand proper wellness practices to live our healthiest and best life!

I am scared about where our country is headed in the next several years. Obesity is currently at an all-time high and statistics are showing 42 percent of American adults may be obese by 2050. Obesity has not only severe health consequences but also economic consequences for our country and other countries around the world. I am concerned about the physical consequences as well as the mental and emotional consequences. Depression and anxiety are more prevalent in overweight and obese individuals. So when I hear the future obesity stats, I know that means there will likely also be an increase of depression and anxiety. I believe that individuals who suffer from depression do not live their lives fully and we have an opportunity to help them combat obesity so they can live amazing lives.

Depression costs our society $210 billion per year as of 2017. Part of my mission in writing this book is to empower people by providing the tools needed to combat obesity and provide insight into better wellness practices. How we feel when we look in the mirror and what we say to ourselves every day is vital to how we live our lives! My hope is that you will discover the tools needed to help you elevate your life and find more balance in your wellness!

Embrace the Journey

I have come to realize that having grace for oneself is key to a healthy wellness journey. It is important to remember that life is going to happen and you cannot let the obstacles that come along stop you from reaching your goals. There were days when my shift ran over or I was stressed with family situations or I was just plain tired. Learning not to be so hard on yourself when things do not go as planned will be incredibly important. I see people fail at reaching their wellness goals because they give up after the first time they fail. Come on, I'm sure you are doing your best! Be kind to yourself and compassionate when you have a setback in life. You probably give plenty of grace and compassion to others—so why not do it for yourself?

I hesitated to write this book for so long. I did not feel I had anything new to offer and I was worried the book would not come out "perfect". Many months went by and this book still remained in my heart but not on paper. You see, I have been extremely guilty of chasing perfection over progress. And it hurt me tremendously. I used to beat myself when I didn't understand something perfectly during medical school and residency. I would beat myself up when I messed up my diet and ate a tub of ice cream and sprinkles. My desire for doing things perfectly stopped me from asking questions. But one day I shifted and I walked away from perfectionism. Walking away from the desire for perfectionism has been vital to my growth. When we choose to chase perfection we are setting ourselves up for failure—and I know that is not what you want to do. Perfect does not exist because there are always ways we can improve or do something better than before. Tony Robbins says that "Perfectionism is the lowest human standard that we can aim for because it doesn't exist". Look to do one thing better every day. Chase progress, not perfection!

The journey to wellness is not a sprint but a marathon. I cannot tell you how many times I wished I could be skinnier or "more fit" really fast. Being healthy is a lifestyle. And notice that the word "life" was stated. I come across many people in the Emergency Room who are willing to try and make changes but only for a limited amount of time. You should not treat yourself well for just three months or six months or just two years—the goal should be to create a healthy foundation you can follow for the rest of your life. I believe you need to make life-long changes and you should know it will take time to reach your goals. Prepare yourself mentally for the fact that you are making changes to your nutrition and self-care that you will carry on for the rest of your life.

Practicing self-awareness and self-reflection has been so important to my wellness journey and my growth as a woman. Self-reflection is something I have always practiced since I was a child. I always look back on the past week and ask what went well and what did not go well. I encourage you to do the same. Look back on the week and note some of the changes you have made and give yourself a score. Think about your strengths and your weaknesses and be honest with yourself. Honesty is everything, especially with yourself. Did you make your wellness a priority? Did you get enough sleep? Was your stress level high? Did you eat well? These are some questions to ask yourself. One practice I have found to be helpful in growing is to look to at people I admire and think about what characteristics they have that I admire. Then working hard within myself to build some of those same characteristics. Becoming more self-aware and identifying your emotional triggers will not only help you with your wellness goals but with your overall life.

Over the years I have learned that you only have three choices in life: Give up, give in or give it all you've got. There will be times in your life that you will want to eat whatever you want and times when you will choose sleep over exercise. There will be times when the stress in your life is very high and you feel like everything is crumbling around you. There will be times when you are scared because the path ahead of you is unknown. Despite all of this you must make it your mantra to "Never Ever Give Up." Your pursuit of health and career goals are so important—never cut yourself short by giving up!

Gossip Kills Trust—Especially in Your Head

Are you your own worst enemy? For many years I would look at myself in the mirror and say "You are fat!" or "I hate my thick thighs" and even at one point I just wanted to "cut" off all the fat from my body. I would say these things to myself while crying and feeling defeated and frustrated. Instead of loving myself—I was doing the opposite. Every time clothes would not fit me in a fitting room I would be disgusted with myself. I avoided photos. I was ashamed to be naked. These thoughts about my body led me to have lower self-esteem and my confidence tanked. I have learned our life becomes a reflection of what we tell ourselves so we must be careful of the words we choose to say. We have such high expectations for ourselves sometimes that we set ourselves up for failure.

Do you have a story that you keep repeating to yourself? What are the words that you are speaking to yourself? Are you repeating "I am fat and no one loves me"? Or are you repeating "I am gorgeous and deserve amazing love"? I told myself I was too busy to workout or I could never follow a proper nutrition plan for a long time. I kept telling myself I was not smart enough because I was a horrible test taker and had a tough time getting into medical school. All a story. All a lie. Setbacks do happen in our lives but they do not have to define us. We can choose how we react to them and especially how long we replay the situation in our head. Make sure you are telling yourself an empowering story and not one that puts you down.

One thing I have found to be certain is our reality is a reflection of our mindset. When I visited a poor village in the Dominican Republic one thing that struck me was how much joy was in the eyes of the people. Ever notice how there are people with no money and limited resources yet they are so happy? Or even the opposite—people with a ton of money and luxury yet incredibly depressed? Those differences are because of their mindset. Our reality is a reflection of our mindset. Are you someone who looks at a glass as half empty or half full? There are different ways of perceiving the world but our perception has a huge effect on how we respond to life. Every day we wake up and get to CHOOSE how we want to feel. We can choose to be happy or sad. We can choose to view ourselves as ugly or beautiful. It all starts in our mind. And yes, shit happens! We cannot avoid obstacles and struggles in life but we can absolutely control how we choose to react to them.

Again, words are incredibly powerful and we must watch what we say to ourselves. Ever notice that talking negatively about ourselves is the easiest thing to do sometimes? I know for a long time I would tell myself "I am not smart enough" and guess what that did? It limited me because I would be afraid to raise my hand in class or give my opinion in conversations. I would speak these words to myself even though I have a degree. Same thing with my body. I would tell myself I was "fat" every time I looked in the mirror. And what did that do? Well, it made me feel less beautiful. What words are you saying to yourself? Are you speaking positivity and love to yourself or are you tearing yourself down?

Gratitude with Some of the F-Word

Over time I have learned to embrace the messiness of life. Life is messy, especially with how we treat ourselves and how we treat others. We all make mistakes. It is important to not beat yourself up when something goes wrong or you make a bad decision. When failure and obstacles arise ask yourself "What can I learn from this?" The lessons we learn about ourselves and others in messy times are the ones with the most wisdom. Embrace it.

Stop being a prisoner of your past. Lack of forgiveness for yourself and others forces you to be stuck at a particular point and time in the past. You cannot successfully navigate the present if you are stuck in the past. Now that is not fair to yourself, is it? By not practicing forgiveness you are acting TODAY in the version of yourself from the PAST. You are not capable of moving forward without practicing forgiveness. Many people are limiting themselves because they have not forgiven themselves or someone else for something that happened in the past. Think of life as a road and you are in the driver's seat. You have two options, you can look out the window in front of you or you can look in the rearview window. Which is bigger? Which allows you to see more of the world? Which gives you MORE direction? Of course the big window right in front of you. When you don't practice forgiveness you are constantly looking in the small rearview window instead of the big window in front. I don't know about you, but that sounds like you may get into an accident.

You may believe that forgiveness is about the other person but actually, it is more for you. Holding on to pain and grudges from the past is negative energy that we are allowing into our current life. You do not deserve that negativity. Your past does not define you but it can serve as a treasure chest of lessons. Be grateful for those lessons because they brought you to where you are today in life. Remember, forgiveness is more for you than for the other person. So let's take some action—if there is someone you have to forgive – do it now. Write them a letter or send them a message saying "I forgive you and you owe me nothing." This letter or message does not need to be mailed if you don't want. This act of forgiveness is done for you, not the other person.

Gratitude is a vital part of an extraordinary life. What is gratitude? Gratitude is the quality or feeling of being thankful. So many people are focused on the negatives in life that they forget the positive things in the life that should be cherished and appreciated. It is one thing to acknowledge the negative, but when you only focus on that you forget about all the other amazing things going on in your life. When you get into the habit of only pointing out the negative things in your life, you are also more prone to not take compliments given to you. For example, instead of bashing your body—glorify it for how it physically helps you get through the day. You have five senses, two legs, two arms, a strong heart, and lungs that function. Your body is actually pretty darn amazing!

Start each day with gratitude and your life will never be the same again. Tony Robbins says, "Trade your expectations for appreciation" and your stress level in life will diminish tremendously and you will be filled with more love. So many people are focused on everything that goes wrong. When your thoughts are focused on gratitude it is hard to feel negative feelings at the same time. Trust me on this. Would you rather be focused on all the bad things going on or would you rather start the day feeling blessed for the amazing things in your life? As I have studied successful people, one thing that is a common practice of many of them is starting their day with three things they are grateful for and ending the day in the same manner.

What are three things you are grateful for at this moment?

Time to Reprogram

You are not broken—you are whole. I hear often from women that they wish they could "fix" this or that about their body or mindset. Or they cannot wait for that "significant other" to make them "whole". Newsflash! You are not broken and do not need to be fixed. AND you do not need someone else to make you whole. Yes, you may need to grow and learn from some valuable obstacles in your life—but you are not broken! All the tools you need for success and happiness are within you. You do not need to wait for the perfect love interest to make you whole. Stop waiting until you are "fixed" or "whole" to LIVE your life! Look within darling because everything you need is within you!

I know I had to stop chasing the wrong feelings. For so long I kept saying that I wanted to be happy all the time. How about you? Are you chasing happiness? Many patients and clients tell me they are down on life or their body because they are not "happy". One thing to understand is that happiness is situational. Instead of waiting only for "happiness" to rule your world, choose to work toward finding inner joy, peace, and contentment. Those are things that you can find within yourself that are not dependent on the people around you.

If I am going to talk about reprogramming then I cannot leave out the law of attraction. I absolutely believe in the law of attraction and feel it has helped me tremendously with my own personal goals. The law of attraction is the idea that what you focus on, whether positive or negative, manifests in your reality. This is incredibly important especially when it comes to your goals and the people and experiences you want in your life. For example, ever noticed how positive people always seem to have other positive people around them? Or, that there are some people who just always seem to have bad luck? Well, this is all based on the law of attraction. So be mindful of your thoughts and what you ask for because your focus, energy, and intentions determine what you will receive. You must remember you will attract and receive what you think about and ask for, whether it is good or bad. The more specific you are in asking for what you want, the more likely you will get it. So, let's take some action. Take out a piece of paper or your journal and write down your desires and goals.

"*Where there is no vision, the people perish.*"
Proverbs 29:18 (KJV)

Vision is everything—a man without a vision will perish. Whenever you get into a car you usually have an idea where you are going so you are able to get to your destination with minimum roadblocks. You are able to map out your route and reach your destination because you have an end-goal in mind—a vision. You also need to have a vision for your life so you can map out your route and determine the steps you need to take to reach your goals—your destination. Visualization is incredibly powerful and if you can imagine, believe and see where you want to go—you will be surprised to see the steps appear right in front of you. However, if you do not know what you want to achieve or where you want to go, no one else will figure that out for you. This is something incredibly empowering because it means you can create the life you dream of! Vision boards are incredibly powerful and something I highly recommend. Sit down and plan what you want to achieve in the next year and create your vision board. Write down your goals and desires and visualize what you want using your own photos and/or pictures from magazines.

What you say to yourself repeatedly will become your reality. This is why affirmations or incantations are so powerful. For a long time, I used to look in the mirror and say "You are fat!" or "You are too curvy" or "You are not smart enough." You can see how those words can be damaging and affected my self-esteem. I had to change the words and reframe them. I had to start finding empowering words. Here are some of my favorite: I am enough! I am worthy! I am beautiful and powerful!

Drive with the Right People

One of the first things I share with people I mentor is to be mindful of who you listen to. A long time ago I heard a quote from renowned businessman and personal development guru, Jim Rohn that was incredibly powerful for me, "you are the average of the five people who you surround yourself with." This has to do with all areas of your life including finances and how you live your life. I believe we should be mindful of who we share our goals with and who we take advice from. I always look for mentors and people who have walked the path

I am trying to reach—and ask them for advice. A lot of people share their dreams with family and friends without even realizing their family and friends may have limiting beliefs within themselves. Your own family and friends can knock down your dreams and vision so you must be selective about who you share and connect with. When I mentor entrepreneurs and they tell me they went to their father who has never owned a business for business advice—I look at them and say, "why would you ask your father who has never owned a business in his life what you should be doing in relation to your business?" You want to ask someone who has experience and who has walked the path. I have been really mindful of my peer group over the last few years and I encourage you to do the same.

Surround yourself with people who have a growth mindset. The worst thing you can do is surround yourself with people who are not growing. You want to be around other people who are setting big goals in their lives and encouraging you to do the same. Talk about visions, goals, and ideas. When you talk to people who are goal oriented you'll be influenced by them and motivated to take your life to the next level as well. You will automatically elevate to new levels of success if you always surround yourself with driven like-minded people.

I caution you to watch for energy drainers on this journey of physical and emotional wellness. Ever notice how when you walk into a room you can feel if there's negative or positive energy? Or ever notice when someone else walks into the room and all of a sudden there's a bad feeling? Those are energy drainers! These are the people in your life that will absolutely suck you dry. You must be very careful and mindful of who these people are so you can make sure to keep them appropriately far away from you. Make sure you surround yourself with positivity and inspiration and not be drained by those who are stuck in a rut. You have to protect your energy—especially when you're trying to make positive changes in your body and your life.

Want to know a tip to improve your chance of success? Never be the smartest person in the room. It is incredibly important to surround yourself with people who can guide you. If you are the most knowledgeable person in your circle, then it's time to find a new circle. You will not grow if you were surrounded by people who know less than you. Seek out friendships and colleagues who know more about what you're trying to achieve and build relationships with them because they will share their knowledge and help you reach your goals faster.

And most importantly, be around people who are honest and tell you the truth. One thing I have always appreciated about myself is that I am very honest and open with those around me. Some people may think I am too harsh and blunt but I tell it how it is. I also make sure to choose friends who will push me and be honest with me. You will not grow if you surround yourself with people who only want to please you. You need people who can be objective and honest with you—even if the truth hurts. Sometimes it's not easy to hear the truth but if you want to change your life and rise to the next level you must be open and willing to hear feedback that could help you.

Building Blocks

A strong foundation is key when it comes to setting yourself up for nutritional success and there is no foundation without first understanding nutritional basics, like macronutrients. I come across many patients in the Emergency Room who think they are eating well-balanced meals but when I dig a little deeper into their meal plans I discover they are very unbalanced. Many people are confused by what types of food are good and how much they should be having.

So what are the macronutrients? By definition, macronutrients are substances that our body needs for energy in large quantities in order to function and survive. The "macros" are where our calories come from and there are three main macronutrients: carbohydrates, proteins, and fats.

Let's chat about those carbs! I know everyone loves carbs and wishes they can eat a ton of them (I know I do at times!) but the truth of the matter is our society is changing and with obesity at an all-time high, this is one macronutrient we need to keep a close eye on. Carbohydrates come in at four calories per gram and are easily broken down and used by our body as a primary fuel source. Carbohydrates break down into glucose and glucose is utilized in our body for energy.

There are two things I want you to pay attention to when it comes to carbohydrates: quality and quantity. Quality has to do with whether they are processed or unprocessed. Quantity has to do with the amount of carbohydrates you are eating per day. Everyone's tolerance of carbohydrates is different which means our bodies are unique in the amount of carbs we should be eating. Not everyone can process the same amount of carbohydrates. For example, if you have polycystic ovarian syndrome or are post-menopausal, you should be limiting your carbohydrate intake. However, if you are an athlete or have a high amount of body muscle, you can usually process more carbohydrates than the average person.

The best carbohydrates overall are slow digesting, unprocessed and have a high amount of fiber. Choose wisely!

An honorable mention has to go to fiber! One of the top complaints from children and adults is abdominal pain and a huge culprit is a nutrition plan low in fiber. Why? Well, fiber is a carbohydrate that our body cannot break down. This is actually good because this allows the nutrient to pass through our digestive tracts whole and take waste products with them. Medical issues like constipation and hemorrhoids are due to a diet low in fiber. The American Heart Association suggests that total dietary fiber intake should be twenty-five to thirty grams a day from food, not supplements. Currently, dietary fiber intake among adults in the United States averages about fifteen grams a day. We absolutely have some improvement to make!

Protein is the next major macronutrient. Proteins are the building blocks of our body. We need protein to build every aspect of our body. Proteins are used to build muscle and bone, repair tissue and cells, and make up our hair and nails. It is important to understand that one gram of protein is equivalent to four calories. Similar to carbohydrates, not everyone should be eating the same amount of protein. Some people try to lose weight by eating a high protein, low carb, and low-fat diet. But that may not be the best plan for you. Too much protein can cause inflammation in the body and can actually lead to weight gain for some people. How much protein you should eat on a daily basis depends on your metabolism, body fat percentage, age, and weight.

Fat is the third major macronutrient. Fat is a major energy source and building block within our body. Fat is especially important for our hormones and our brain cells. One gram of fat is equal to nine calories. I will discuss fat is more detail in the next chapter because it is vital to our nutrition and wellness.

Eat Fat—It's Good for You!

We need to "unbrainwash" ourselves when it comes to fat. There is a common misconception that all fat is bad for you and will make you *fat*. This is far from the truth and there has been misinformation put out in the past around this subject. So what happened? There was a low-fat craze back in the 1980s and 1990s. I remember low-fat everything growing up. I believe the low-fat craze was a key factor in today's obesity epidemic because we replaced quality fats in our diets with processed carbs and sugars—which has been the most damaging to our health. Fortunately, scientific evidence is showing that high-fat diets are better than low-fat diets for weight loss and for reversing heart disease risk, diabetes, high blood pressure and so much more (1). The evidence also shows there is no link between dietary fat, saturated fat, or cholesterol, and heart disease (2).

So let's talk fat basics. Dietary fats break down into fatty acids once digested. There are two main types of fatty acids: unsaturated and saturated. Fatty acids are joined together to create triglycerides, which are the major form of fat found in the diet and the major storage form of fat found in our body. Monounsaturated and polyunsaturated fats are the most commonly known good fats. Saturated fats are still needed in our diet but best consumed in moderation. One thing to also keep in mind is our genetics do play a role in how our bodies process saturated fats and some people are more prone to weight gain and disease when consuming them. Omega-3 and omega-6 fats are both polyunsaturated fats that are important for our health. It is vital to have a balance of unsaturated and saturated fats in our nutrition for optimal health. Disease can occur when there is an imbalance.

Dietary fat also plays a role in your cholesterol levels. Now let me just clarify—cholesterol itself isn't bad. Your body needs cholesterol to function properly. But just like most things, it can negatively affect your health when you get too much of it. HDL cholesterol is the "good" kind of cholesterol found in your blood. LDL cholesterol is the "bad" kind. The key is to keep HDL levels high and LDL levels low. Why? Because high HDL levels protect against heart disease and stroke while high levels of LDL can clog arteries and increase heart disease. The best way to improve your cholesterol profile is to replace bad fats with quality fats.

So how is fat good for your body? Well, our body loves to use fat for energy and some parts of our body prefer fat for fuel over glucose. Our body needs fat for many functions throughout our body. Fat helps to manufacture and balance our hormones. Fat is a building block in our cell membranes and vital to our brain and nervous systems.

Fat helps to transport the fat-soluble vitamins A, D, E and K. Research shows that omega-3 fatty acids reduce inflammation and may help lower risk of chronic diseases such as heart disease, cancer, and arthritis.

Quality is most important when it comes to fat intake. One of the benefits of fat is it helps you stay full longer when added to your food. Fat also adds a ton of flavor to your food! I am not saying to go out to McDonald's and get three cheeseburgers! When it comes to fat—quality does matter! The key to increasing your fats is to focus on natural fats that are good for you. A short selection of quality fats includes grass-fed and hormone free protein, fish, eggs, nuts and seeds, vegetables, olive oil, coconut oil, grass-fed butter, full-fat dairy, and avocado.

Most diets today are high in omega-6 fats causing a dangerous imbalance with omega-3 fats. Ideally, the balance between omega-6 and omega-3 should be a 1:1 ratio. However, many people have a 16:1 ratio. This imbalance comes from the high consumption of omega-6 fats in our diet. Omega-6 fat food sources include corn oil, safflower oil and meat from animals that are fed corn. It is important to increase your omega-3 fats and reduce your omega-6 fats. Good sources of omega-3 fatty acids include fatty fish such as salmon, mackerel, and sardines, flaxseeds, walnuts, canola oil, and unhydrogenated soybean oil.

You also need to be cautious about trans fats. These fats are processed in a way that allows them to harden at room temperature and allow foods to have a longer shelf life. A high trans fat intake is associated with higher risk of heart disease, cancer, Alzheimer's disease, and lymphoma. Trans fats also lower HDL, the good cholesterol and increase LDL, the bad cholesterol. Some common sources of trans fat are found in pastries, cookies, doughnuts, muffins, cakes, pizza dough, Stick margarine, and vegetable shortening.

Your Favorite Drug—Sugar

Sugar can be found in so many different places in the western diet and I believe it is one of the key players in obesity. Yes, all that sugar you love is making you fat and making you sick.

I would like to explain the different types of sugar. Sugar is found in natural whole foods but also added to foods to make them sweet. Simple sugars are made up of sucrose, glucose, and fructose.

Glucose is the broken down molecule from carbohydrates. Glucose is one of two main energy sources that our body can use. The other energy source is ketones, which are energy molecules that come from fat metabolism. Sucrose is your typical table sugar and is what you find in candy and sweets. Sucrose breaks down into glucose and fructose. The glucose is then used by our muscles and brain for energy and the fructose is metabolized in the liver.

Fructose is a sugar found naturally in fruits and vegetables. Excess sugar that our body does not utilize for immediate energy is stored in our body as fat. Sugar is a key factor in insulin resistance. Insulin is a hormone our body releases in response to glucose in the bloodstream. Insulin's role is to help cells in our body remove glucose from the bloodstream so it can be used for immediate energy or stored as fat. Whenever we eat a meal high in carbs or processed sugar, that food will get broken down into glucose in our bloodstream. Insulin then sees all this glucose in the bloodstream and says "Hey! We have all this glucose that we need to remove and store." But after a while, insulin needs to see MORE glucose in the bloodstream before it does anything with it. In a sense they get resistant to small amounts of glucose and need large amounts before it does anything—this is called insulin resistance.

I have come to learn from my own experience that fruit is nature's candy. Just like everything else, moderation is vital when it comes to our nutrition. The old saying "an apple a day keeps the doctor away" is still true but an "acai bowl a day" is not the same thing. People eat too much fruit today and think it is ok because it comes from nature. However, sugar is still sugar, even if it comes from fruit. Fructose is the main sugar in fruit. Fructose cannot be used for energy by our muscles and brain and goes straight to the liver to be metabolized. I want you to pay close attention to what I just said. I was shocked when I learned that fructose is not utilized by any of our cells for energy—yet we eat so much fruit! Fructose is stored in the form of glycogen in the liver. Once the glycogen storage is full in the liver, the rest gets stored as fat. This storage of fat occurs both in the liver and on the body. This process is why increased amounts of fructose intake can lead to fatty liver disease.

Sugar in excess causes some major problems in our body. One that you may not be familiar with is inflammation. Lots of sugar intake can cause total body inflammation. I must first introduce you to AGE, Advanced Glycogen End products, in order to understand how. AGE's are a normal byproduct of metabolism and AGE's contribute to oxidative stress and inflammation in our body. This inflammation can then lead to diabetes and cardiovascular disease. So when we eat a lot of sugar our body produces more AGEs, which can be destructive to our health.

Sugar also acts like an addictive drug. Ever have those days when you CRAVE something sweet? I used to have them all the time, especially after a long stressful day in the ER! When I would indulge in something sweet I would feel so happy! And when I did cave in I also ate way more than I had planned. Does that happen to you? Well, sugar is addictive and acts like a drug in our brain. Our brain actually processes sugar like a reward and our brain gets a dose of dopamine when we eat sugar. Dopamine is the "happy chemical" in our brain that drug users also get when they take their drug. So, yes it is hard to come off of sugar because your body is actually addicted to it. As an ex-sugar addict, I am here to tell you that with a well-balanced nutrition plan and also understanding WHY you reach for the sugar—you CAN break the addiction!

Eat All Your Damn Food

Have you been following a nutrition plan and wondering why you are not seeing results? It could be how much food you are eating. I have struggled with knowing how MUCH to eat and having a fear of eating too much. For so long, I was afraid to eat more than 1,200 calories because I believed I would not lose weight if I ate more than 1,200 calories a day. Boy, was I wrong! Actually, I was not eating ENOUGH calories for my body and I have learned that most people do not eat enough for their body weight. Our bodies are complex intricate machines that work at a cellular level. Just like a car needs gas in order to function—we need fuel in order to operate at our best. Our fuel is the food we eat and the calories come from the food. Our bodies are smart machines and built to survive—when we do not eat enough food—our metabolism adapts so that it can function on fewer calories. Our body will then hold on to body fat because it is unsure it will have enough nutrients the next time you eat. Underfeeding ourselves is how we truly mess up our metabolism. We all have a baseline energy requirement that our bodies need in order to function and survive at its highest quality. An understanding of this energy requirement is essential to accomplishing your wellness goals.

So let's break down your basic energy requirements and what it means. Every cell in our body requires energy to function. Breathing, thinking, our heart beating, our muscles moving are just some of the many functions our body needs the energy to perform. We get energy from the food that we put into our body. All food contains energy in the form of calories. So what are calories? Technically, a calorie is a unit of heat measurement. But more simply, it is the amount of energy a food provides. We all have a minimum level of energy our body uses to maintain our vital functions and this is called our Basal Metabolic Rate (BMR). In other words, your BMR is the energy your body needs just to survive twenty-four hours if it were sitting on a couch ALL day doing absolutely nothing! Interestingly, your BMR accounts for 70 percent of the energy we expend. Your body works HARD to Survive!

So how do you calculate your BMR? A rough way to calculate it is using the Harris-Benedict equation that was revised by Mifflin and St Jeor in 1990:

For men: BMR = 10 x weight (kg) + 6.25 x height (cm) – 5 x age (years) + 5

For women: BMR = 10 x weight (kg) + 6.25 x height (cm) – 5 x age (years) – 16

So for example: Let's take a 155-pound woman who is 5'8 and 33 years old.

155 pounds is 70.4 kg. 5'8 is 176.784 cm. BMR = (10 x 70.4) + (6.25 x 176.784)—(5 x 33)—161 = 1,482 calories

One thing to keep in mind is that no equation is perfect. Based on this example, the woman above would need 1,482 calories just to perform her body's basic functions. And this does not even include exercise or regular physical activity.

So let's understand your requirements for your specific goals. We all have different goals. Some of us want to lose weight and some of us want to gain weight. Some want to drop body fat and some want to build muscle or do a combination of both! You need to make sure you are eating enough to fuel yourself in order to see results and reach your individual goals. It is important to find the balance between your calorie intake (food) and your calorie expenditure (physical activity) needed to reach your goals. Before learning what your body needs—it's important to understand that a pound of body fat is equal to 3500 calories. To lose a pound you need to create a deficit of 3500 calories by either eating fewer calories or exercising more. And to gain a pound you need to create a surplus of 3500 calories.

Continuing to use the Harris-Benedict Equation we can figure out how much energy your body needs on a daily basis including your physical activity.

How to Determine your Recommended Daily Intake of Calories based on your Activity.

This chart is adapted from the Harris Benedict Equation.

Little to no Exercise	Calories = BMR X 1.2
Light exercise (1-3 days per week)	Calories = BMR x 1.375
Moderate exercise (3-5 days per week)	Calories = BMR x 1.55
Heavy Exercise (6-7 days per week)	Calories = BMR x 1.725
Very Heavy Exercise (twice per day)	Calories = BMR x 1.9

Now once you know your daily energy requirements you can calculate the amount of calories needed to lose weight or gain weight. In order to lose weight, you would subtract 500 calories daily and in order to gain weight, you would add 500 calories daily.

So let us take the example of our woman from before. Her BMR was 1,482 calories. Let's say that she does light exercise twice a week – I would multiply her 1,482 calories x 1.375 and that would give me a total calorie count of 2,037. In order to lose weight, I would subtract 500 calories from 2,037 which gives me 1,537. Therefore, this women woman would need to eat 1,537 calories every day to lose weight.

So let's take some action: Take out a piece of paper and use the formula above to calculate your BMR and your daily calorie requirements based on your physical activity level. This will give you a rough estimate of where to begin to start eating for your goals!

Also, don't be scared by the idea of having to count calories forever. I do not want you to do that at all! I do want you to have an idea of the general amount of calories your body needs to reach your goals. Once you have those calories in mind you can practice portion control. Portion control is an important method that can be used for your wellness goals, especially weight loss goals. All foods have suggested serving sizes and it is important to become knowledgeable about this. A lot of times we eat with our eyes anyway—I know I do! So it's important to re-train your eyes to know how much you should be eating. And this takes time! In the beginning, you can use food scales or measuring cups to portion out your servings. You can even use an app to keep track of your food. There are many on the market to use! The long-term goal for you is to have a general idea of what the right "amount" of food looks like for your body for your goals.

Intermittent Fasting

I wanted to touch upon intermittent fasting because it has absolutely been vital to my success. This is just one approach to eating and it is important that you find what works best for you. I found that by following this style of eating I was able to lower my body fat percentage and lose weight easier than the conventional three to four square meals a day.

So what is intermittent fasting? Intermittent fasting is an eating pattern and NOT a diet. You alternate between a period of fasting and a period of eating with this pattern. You still eat all of your calories your body needs but only within a certain timeframe, which is called your "eating window." For example, you will eat within an eight-hour "eating window" and then fast for sixteen hours. This is called a 16:8 protocol, fasting for sixteen hours straight and then an eating window of eight hours straight. A typical schedule for this would be to eat from 12 pm to 8 pm and then fast from 8 pm to 12 pm the next day. When you choose to start your eating window doesn't matter as long as you follow the 16:8 protocol, so you can figure out a time frame that best works for you. This is clearly different than eating every three to four hours throughout the day, which is what most people, tell you to do.

There are three main ways you can start with intermittent fasting: alternate day fasting, once per week fasting, and daily fasting. Alternate day fasting is when you fast for a full twenty-four hours and then eat your calories within the next twenty-four hours and alternate that pattern. Once per week fasting is when you choose one day of the week to fast for a full twenty-four hours and then eat your normal nutrition plan the rest of the week. Since I am a proponent of gradually starting things I recommend the daily fasting. There are two main protocols you can follow for daily fasting, the 16:8 protocol or the 20:4 protocol.

I would suggest starting with the 16:8 Protocol: Choose a six to eight-hour eating window and fast the rest of the day. So you will do a sixteen-hour fast with an eight-hour eating window period. Ideally, you want to fast for at least sixteen hours to really start seeing the benefits of intermittent fasting. My recommendation is to start with a large eating window like eight hours and slowly shorten that window. In the beginning, you will be very hungry by the time you reach your eating window. However, your body will get used to this style of eating and the more you do it the more your body will adapt. You will know when you can transition to a shorter eating window when you are not feeling as hungry by hour sixteen of your fast and feel you can push it another hour or two for a full eighteen hour fast.

What I love about intermittent fasting are the many benefits. First, your body will burn fat! When you put your body into fasting mode it gives your body the opportunity to tap into stored fat, especially your stubborn body fat! When you are eating all day you are constantly increasing your insulin levels—which is not good because insulin helps you store fat. Also, having high insulin levels for long periods of time leads to diabetes, inflammation, heart disease and possibly cancer. If you are always eating, you are not giving your body the ability to tap into the stored fat and instead burning what you are eating throughout the day. In others words, you burn stored body FAT when you are fasting and you burn food when you are eating.

Intermittent fasting helps to regulate your blood sugar during the day. It helps in our ability to respond better to the hormones in our body. It helps to release growth hormones, which help you burn fat. It also helps to regulate blood glucose, control blood lipids, and decreases total body inflammation.

Focus on food quality and continue regular exercise when you are implementing intermittent fasting.

Body

Take Responsibility

When I finally made a decision to take my nutrition more seriously during residency I knew I had to own my actions and stop putting the blame on external factors. Do you feel you give up quickly on your goals? Or how about specifically when it comes to weight loss goals? Do you feel you give up too fast because of lack of results? Most people do not own their actions or take responsibility for their lack of results. It is not someone else's fault if you do not reach your goals—it is your life and your choices. Instead of looking at other people to solve your problems you need to look within yourself.

If you do not eat well, then you will not see the results you want. I see a lot of women who want to eat all their favorite foods and still see amazing results. When it comes to improving your relationship with food it must be understood that it is truly a lifestyle change. And like any change it takes time.

You cannot expect to go out to dinner and eat the whole bread basket and have a glass of wine and then step on the scale the next day and see weight loss. Be realistic and do not set the wrong expectations. I'm not saying you can't enjoy food and your experiences but just realize your choices will determine the results. When I go out to eat and indulge in some amazing bread and dessert—I am not disillusioned to believe I'm going to feel freaking amazing the next day! I know I will feel bloated and I will have to drink a ton of water for the next few days to reverse the effects of that choice.

It is also important to make exercise a habit. Our bodies are not meant to remain stagnant. Our bodies are meant to be moving and challenging itself on a daily basis. Most people are sitting in an office and in the car for long commute times, never really getting any physical activity in. This is why a consistent schedule of exercise within your week is incredibly important for your body and your physiology. Whether you want to lose weight or simply improve the strength of your body—exercise absolutely has to be a part of the plan. And yes, I know there will be days when you do not want to exercise, like when you are on vacation. But I want to encourage you to look at exercise as preventative medicine. If you were going on vacation and you had to take certain medications, just because you were on vacation doesn't mean that you will stop taking your medications, correct? Well, exercise is your medicine, it's your medicine to prevent disease in your body and improve your health. You must make it a habit.

Do not be surprised if you do not see results after days of poor choices. Being healthy and taking your life to another level is a habit. And like any habit, it needs to be repeatedly practiced. You should not take any days off when it comes to your health. Yes, I understand there may be times when you are incredibly stressed out or you are tired or you just do not feel like doing it, but you must push through anyway. Sometimes things are out of our control and we have a small setback but the key is to get back on track as quickly as we can. Do not beat yourself up if after days or even weeks or even months of making poor food choices and not exercising you read a number that is high on the scale or have clothes that do not fit. You are not a failure but your actions are what led to this outcome. You need to change your actions if you want different results.

Mindful Eating

It's time to break up with food that is no longer serving you. Just like you would not stay in a relationship that is hurting you—why would you continue to put things into your body that are making you unhealthy and making you fat? You have the power and it's time to say goodbye. Just like any breakup, I know it will be tough but you will feel so much freer if you can break the hold food has on you.

Our connection with food is so emotional which is why it can be difficult to eat healthily. So many women eat based on emotions including anger, sadness, happiness, frustration, disappointment, and boredom. Which one of these can you relate to? Making changes in the way you eat takes time because the connection to food is based on emotions the majority of the time. But turning to food for comfort is most likely not serving you.

It is important to pay attention to the right cues. There is a difference between emotional cravings and true hunger. Emotional cravings are when you suddenly feel like eating a bag of chips and a tub of ice cream because you're sad or feeling frustrated. Emotional cravings are when you are at a party and want to indulge in the chips and cheese and wine—even though you're not hungry. It is incredibly important to start listening to your body so you can learn when it's really hungry versus when it's just a craving. True hunger is that discomfort in your stomach when you have not eaten for a few hours and your energy is diminishing and maybe you are even feeling cranky. Learning to listen and deciphering whether you have an emotional craving or a true hunger takes time but I encourage you to develop this understanding of yourself.

I also want to encourage you to really pay attention to your body when you start a nutrition plan. Once you start eliminating all of the garbage and junk you have been feeding your body, it will start speaking to you. Your body will tell you what doesn't serve it and what her problem foods are. The key is to keep your eyes open to it and to make the connection between how you're feeling and what you're eating. For example, when I am at work in the emergency room and I eat a meal that is high in carbohydrates within an hour I feel incredibly sluggish and want to take a nap. It does not matter whether or not I had enough sleep the night before – the sluggish feeling is a result of the amount of carbohydrates I had. So if I were to listen to my body—it is telling me not to eat as many carbohydrates if I want to have more energy. For you, there may be certain foods that cause discomfort and bloating in your stomach. I want you to make sure you make the connection between different foods and how you are feeling. I believe when you are able to truly have a better understanding of what foods give you energy and make you feel amazing, then you will be more likely to want to eat those foods and develop a better nutritional plan for yourself. Understanding your body and knowing what foods work best for it is priceless.

Now, let's talk about the scale. I used to let the scale rule my life. I remember there were times when I would step on the scale, feel disappointed in the number I saw, and then change all of my plans for the evening just because I no longer wanted to go out. If there's one practice I can encourage you to begin—it is to step away from the scale. The scale does not show the true picture when it comes to reaching your physical fitness goals. When you focus solely on the scale you will potentially become frustrated because the number on the scale fluctuates based on water, whether or not you're on your menstruation and even stress. I like to use the scale as a guide to show me I am heading in the right direction. I prefer to use photographs and measuring tape when it comes to gauging progress so I can see the differences more objectively.

Water

As a busy Physician in the ER it can be tough to stay hydrated. However, I find that when I do not stay on top of my water intake, I am more tired and sluggish throughout the day. My mental clarity also takes a hit when I am dehydrated. Water makes up 60 percent of our body. And usually by the time we feel thirsty we are already dehydrated by one to two percent.

Water is important for so many functions of our body. It has a role in growth processes within our body because it acts as a transporter for many of the building blocks our body needs. Water is an important mineral source and a temperature regulator. For example, when our body overheats, we sweat. Water is a lubricator, which is very important for our joints. It is especially important for our kidney function. Our kidneys process two-hundred quarts of blood daily, eliminating wastes our body does not need. We would not have proper waste elimination without enough water.

Water is also beneficial for weight loss. I know there were many instances when I thought I was hungry when in fact, I was dehydrated. Water also makes you feel full which helps you eat fewer calories throughout the day. Water is also a great energy booster. Sometimes when I feel tired in the middle of a shift, a nice glass of cold water wakes me right back up!

Water is also important in our immunity. When patients come in sick with viruses and common colds, I tell them to go home, rest, and drink plenty of fluids. Drinking water helps with clearing toxins in our body. Water is also fantastic for headaches. One of the top reasons why children and adults suffer from headaches is because of dehydration so make sure to stay properly hydrated. You can also drink too much fluids—which is why it is important that you drink what is appropriate for your body.

As a rule of thumb, it is best to drink half your weight in pounds in ounces. For example, I weigh 155 pounds so I should drink at least 77 ounces of water on a daily basis for optimal health. So let's take some action: Calculate your daily water intake with this formula: Weight (pounds) divided by 2 = water (ounces). Some best practices when it comes to water intake is drinking at least 8–10 ounces as soon as you wake up in the morning, keeping a water bottle with you at all times, and adding fresh cut fruit and lemon to your water.

Movement

Movement is so important to our wellness. Today, most people are spending most of the day sitting on the couch or sitting at a desk instead of moving their body. Our bodies were made to move, they were made to walk, they were made to run and they were made to dance! Making movement an important of my day has been key to finding balance in my wellness. Movement not only helps with weight control but has many other amazing benefits.

Many people get their movement predominantly through exercise. Exercise is an amazing stress reducer. Going for a long walk helps me whenever I feel stressed with work. Exercise also improves your mood. I always feel happy and accomplished after a good sweat session. Exercise is also key to preventing disease in our body and also sometimes reversing conditions like high blood pressure and diabetes. Exercise is also important for your sex life since water improves energy levels and can improve your physical appearance.

When I seriously started making wellness a priority in my life back in 2013, I knew exercise would have to be a major player in my life. With my hectic residency schedule of seventy hours a week, I made time for daily exercise and I made no excuses. Some days were easy and some days I had no desire but I kept a mantra in my head and constantly reminded myself "something is better than nothing" and always made time every day. I encourage you to create an exercise routine that suits your schedule. There is no RIGHT schedule to follow. There is no PERFECT exercise that you need to do. Honestly, whatever schedule you can consistently commit to is just fine! If you can do 30 minutes every day, then wonderful. If you can do 45 minutes three times a week, then fantastic! If you prefer group exercise, find a gym close to you that you will enjoy. The key is to do something!

One mindset shift that was KEY to my long-term success was the decision to work out for strength and NOT pounds lost. Usually, when we start a workout routine, we do it to lose weight. I used to judge my progress by the number on the scale and that was detrimental. As previously discussed, the number on the scale has many factors contributing to it (including water weight, stress, menstruation, etc.) so your focus should not be the numbers on the scale. I made the shift to focusing on improving my strength every day with my workouts. I focused on better form and increasing the weights I used – and this was a much healthier way to judge my progress. I urge you to consider making the same mindset switch.

It is important that you take time to MOVE while you are working too. Take a break every 45—50 minutes when you are working to get up and walk around. That movement gives your brain a short break and revitalizes your body. In fact, I encourage dance parties with yourself! At least once a day, turn on your favorite song and dance like no one is watching. Movement creates energy in our body!

Sleep

Adequate sleep is so important to a healthy lifestyle. This is one area I have always done my best to stay on top of. I personally need about nine hours of sleep to feel rested. What about you? The National Heart, Lung and Blood Institute recommends seven to eight hours for adults. When it comes to children, most guidelines say school-age children should get at least ten hours of sleep a night, and teenagers, nine to ten hours of sleep.

There are two types of sleep: REM and non-REM sleep and both are equally important. REM stands for Rapid Eye Movement and REM sleep is our deeper sleep and when we dream. The two types of sleep happen in cycles throughout our sleep. Our ability to feel rested and function throughout the day depends on whether we get enough total sleep and whether we get enough of each type of sleep.

Sleep is such a vital part of our health. It is important for learning and for our memory. When we sleep our brain is working to create new pathways from what we learned the day before. Sleep is important for healing within our body and also with the function of our hormones that make us feel hungry and full. Sleep also helps with our creativity and mental clarity. Ever notice how after a good night's rest you figure out the answer to a problem much easier?

Sleep deficiency is linked to many chronic diseases. This is because when we sleep, our body is busy repairing vital functions in our body. For example, chronic sleep deficiency can lead to heart disease, high blood pressure, obesity, and depression. Sleep deficiency also causes many car accidents as many people are not as alert on the road.

There are several ways to improve the quality of your sleep. Having a sleep routine is key. This is difficult for me because I am a shift worker so I do not have a set schedule, but going to sleep at the same time every day is best. Having an hour of quiet time before sleep also helps. Eliminating televisions, computers, and phones from the bedroom are also important as the light from these devices keep your brain awake. Avoiding heavy meals and exercise within a couple hours of sleep will help you sleep better.

1. Systematic Review of Randomized controlled trials of low carbohydrate vs low fat in the management of obesity and its comorbidities. Obesity Rev. 2009 Jan; 10(1): 36–50.

2. Association of dietary, circulating, and supplement fatty acids with coronary risk: a systematic review and meta-analysis. Ann Intern Med. 2014 Mar 18; 160 (6): 398–406.

Conclusion

Your wellness needs to be a priority in your life.

As you can see, wellness is not just physical but also emotional, mental and spiritual. The lessons and knowledge I have shared in this book have been key to my success in discovering self-love through self-care. By applying these mindset principles and improving my nutrition and exercise I was able to fully embrace and love who I am—curves and all.

My hope is that something I shared in this book will help you on your journey.

Remember, you are here for a reason and you have gifts that you are meant to share with the world.

Believe in yourself and let your beautiful inner light shine brightly onto others!

And of course, chase Progress not Perfection.

Much Light and Love to You!

Thank You

I want to thank you for purchasing this book and taking the time to read it. I am beyond humbled you made it this far in the book and I truly hope you learned something new and the guidance here will serve you well. These words come from my heart and are truly a glimpse into what has worked for me. Please reach out to me and share what you think of this book and if you feel it can serve others, then I appreciate you sharing it with those you know.

I keep my schedule jam-packed with working in the Emergency Room and working with clients individually and in groups. And I have some exciting news, I will soon be launching an exclusive online program, traveling doing speaking engagements, and releasing a children's book! So let's stay connected.

You can follow me on my social media platforms:

Website: healthyerdoc.com

Facebook: https://www.facebook.com/healthyerdoc/

Instagram: https://www.instagram.com/healthyerdoc/

LinkedIn: www.linkedin.com/in/healthyerdoc

Google+: https://plus.google.com/+Healthyerdoc

YouTube: https://www.youtube.com/c/DrStephanieBurgos

About the Author

Dr. Stephanie Burgos, aka the HealthyER Doc, is a highly acclaimed emergency medicine physician and the founder and CEO of HealthyER Doc and HealthyER You Project, where she uses her platform to teach people how to live a healthy lifestyle and balance their mental, physical and spiritual needs. Dr. Burgos has seen the devastating effects of leading an unhealthy life firsthand in the ER and has made it her mission to help others "Live Life at a Higher Level," using her charismatic bedside manner, optimistic outlook, and positive spirit.

Dr. Burgos is a graduate of Boston College, where she earned a bachelor of science degree. She then earned her doctor of medicine from the University of Medicine and Dentistry of New Jersey and completed her internship and residency at Harvard.

Currently residing in Orlando, Florida, with her life partner, Luc, Dr. Burgos enjoys traveling, food and dance.

To connect, visit her website at
healthyerdoc.com

CPSIA information can be obtained
at www.ICGtesting.com
Printed in the USA
FFOW01n2010010418
46128848-47190FF